LOVE THE EARTH!

by Annalisa Suid
Illustrated by Marilynn G. Barr

For Gregory

Publisher: Roberta Suid
Editor: Murray Suid
Design: Jeffrey Goldman
Production: Santa Monica Press
Educational Consultant: Catherine Dilts

Also by the author: *Holiday Crafts*

The Kids in the Neighborhood © Marilynn G. Barr
Reprinted by permission.

Entire contents copyright © 1993 by Monday Morning Books, Inc.,
Box 1680, Palo Alto, California 94302

For a complete catalog, write to the address above.

Monday Morning is a trademark of
Monday Morning Books, Inc.

Permission is hereby granted to reproduce
student materials in this book for non-commercial
individual or classroom use.

ISBN 1-87829-48-3

Recycled Paper

Printed in the United States of America

9 8 7 6 5 4 3 2 1

CONTENTS

Introduction	4
How to Use This Book	5
Teaching the Basics	6

Literature Links
The Desert Is Theirs	7
Earthmaker Hand	8
Over in the Meadow	9
Firefly Fun	10
A River Ran Wild	11
River Displays	12
The Great Kapok Tree	13
Rain Forest Music	14
The Little House	15
3-D City and Country Murals	16

Environmental Awareness
Scavenger Hunt	17
Nature Hunt Checklist 1	18
Nature Hunt Checklist 2	19
Erosion Exploration	20
Conservation Counts	21
Conservation Counts Chart	22
Save the Air	23

Kid-Made Displays
What the Rain Forest Knows	24
Rain Forest Animal Patterns	25
Rain Forest Facts	26
Saguaro Cactus Time Line	27
Personal Time Line	28
Meadow Mementos Mobile	29
Meadow Patterns	30
Clean Ocean/Dirty Ocean	31
Clean Ocean Patterns	32
Dirty Ocean Patterns	33

Show Time
Program	34
The Great Saguaro Cactus	35
Cactus Costume	36
Rain Forest Rock	37
Jingling Branches	38
Over by the Water	39
Save the Meadowlands Hula	40
Leis and Grass Skirts	41
Flower Patterns	42
Grand Finale	43

Reaching Out
Eco-Newsletter	44
Newsletter Pattern	45
Letter to the Earth	46
Addresses	47
Letter Form	48

INTRODUCTION

We are all neighbors sharing planet Earth. Some people simply go about their business, believing that they can't make any real changes. But you're different! Just picking up this book proves that you care.

Love the Earth! is about encouraging children to value and protect the many kinds of environments that make up the world—from the rain forests to the meadowlands, from deserts to our cities, and from lakes to seas.

As a teacher, you will have a lasting effect on future generations. By offering in-depth information to an eager, creative, and open-minded audience, you can raise the consciousness of these youngsters, while giving them the tools to make changes in the way we treat the environment.

Love the Earth! includes a multitude of integrated-learning activities that can help children to:
- Learn about the many different forms of life that are found in each type of environment;
- Recognize the importance of undisturbed habitats for all living creatures;
- Grasp the concepts of erosion, water pollution, energy conservation, and other environmental processes;
- Relate ecological issues to the entire curriculum and to the development of responsibility and citizenship.

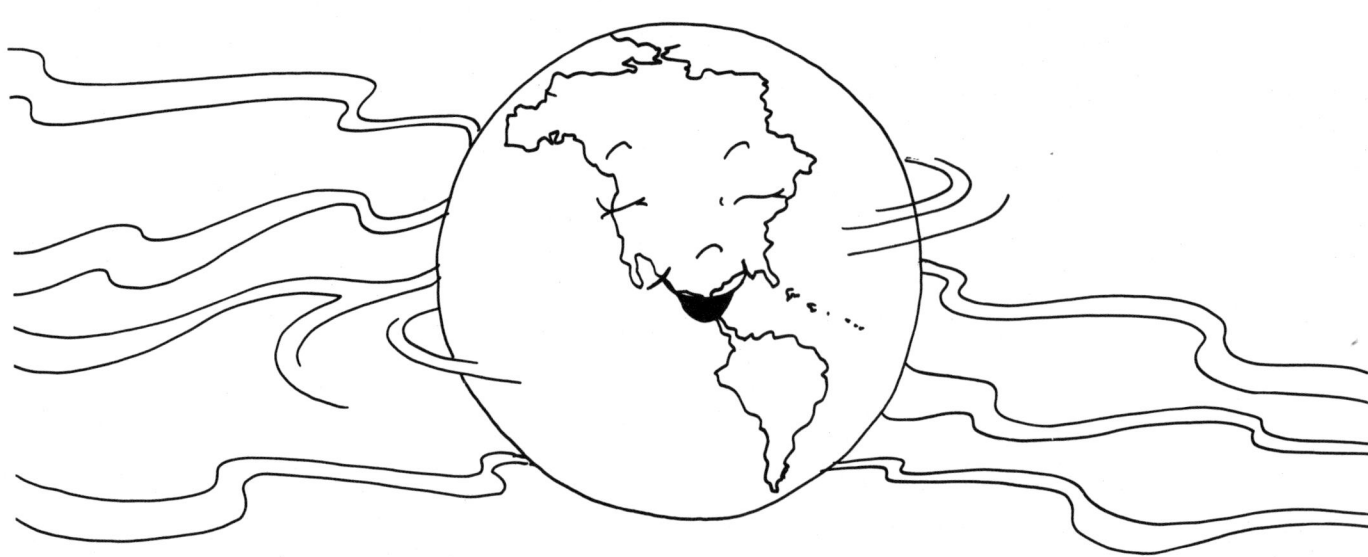

©1993 *Monday Morning Books, Inc.*

HOW TO USE THIS BOOK

Love the Earth! is divided into five sections:

Literature Links focuses on fiction and nonfiction picture books that introduce information about different types of environments: deserts, rain forests, rivers, cities, and meadows. Crafts, projects, and language activities help children make imaginative connections with places that they may not experience in their regular routines.

Environmental Awareness uses the children's own world as a setting for hands-on ecological study. These science-oriented projects are simple, authentic, and fun!

Kid-Made Displays, such as bulletin boards, time lines, exhibits, mobiles, and other eye-catching creations enable children to share what they learn about the Earth with other classes.

Show Time presents songs and costumes to be used in an ecologically oriented program. The pieces bring environmental issues to the children's level. Your students can put on a performance for other classes or parents.

Reaching Out involves students in ecological action through community-oriented projects such as letter writing, and newsletter publishing.

The two bonus posters can be used to introduce this environmental unit as well as to decorate the classroom. Certain activities in this book refer to information provided on the posters.

The main goal is to help your students learn about, explore, and appreciate the environment. As a group, they will make their world cleaner, healthier, and more livable for themselves and their neighbors. The idea is to change the world, and what better place to start than at home?

©1993 Monday Morning Books, Inc.

LOVE THE EARTH!

TEACHING THE BASICS

Your students need to grasp certain concepts in order to understand various environmental problems. The following background information may prove useful in maximizing the value of the activities in this book.

Air Pollution: Harmful gasses produced by cars and factories cause air pollution. Today, many scientists fear that too much carbon dioxide is being produced. Polluted air is bad for people, animals, plants, and trees. Trees can absorb carbon dioxide. However, billions of trees are being cut down. The "Save the Air" activity in the "Environmental Awareness" section describes how planting a tree can help clean the air.

Conservation: We waste a lot of energy. Consider the following facts:
- In one year, people use up the amount of fossil fuel it took one million years to produce.
- Although the United States has five percent of the world's population, it uses over one quarter of the world's oil.
- More energy leaks through American windows every year than flows through the Alaskan pipeline as oil.

The world's energy problem can be reduced through conservation. There are easy ways to save energy on a day-to-day basis. If every household in the United States lowered its average heating temperature six degrees for 24 hours, we could save more than 570,000 barrels of oil. Introduce students to this concept with the "Conservation Counts" activity.

Erosion: This natural process caused by rain and floods involves the washing away of the top layer of the Earth. However, misuse of land—for example, by clear-cutting trees—can increase the loss of the top soil required for plant growth. This type of erosion occurs when plant roots, which hold soil in place, are destroyed and nothing is left to anchor the soil. Luckily, intelligent land management limits erosion. The "Erosion Exploration" project in the "Environmental Awareness" section can help children understand the process of erosion.

Water Pollution: Water is a precious resource—all life on Earth depends on it. Unfortunately, much of our water has become polluted. The dumping of garbage and poisonous chemicals pollutes our rivers, lakes, and oceans. Harmful fertilizers used by farmers or gardeners can drain through the soil and pollute underground water sources. The "Clean Ocean/Dirty Ocean" project will illustrate the need to save our seas.

©1993 Monday Morning Books, Inc.

THE DESERT IS THEIRS

Story:
Byrd Baylor's *The Desert Is Theirs* (Scribner's) describes the difficult life of the Papago Indians, who call the desert home. Known as the "Desert People," this tribe survives in the harsh climate by treating their land "the way you'd treat an old friend." The Indians learn from the neighboring animals, who range from the proud coyote to the tiny scorpion. The Papago respect these animals, believing that the desert creatures have a great understanding about how to make the most of their environment.

Environmental Connection:
Although fiction, this book introduces important environmental concepts that can help children understand and appreciate the bonds between animals and humans.

Language Extension:
Show your class *Clementina's Cactus* by Ezra Jack Keats (Viking), and allow them to make up stories to go with the pictures. Then provide drawing supplies for students to create their own environmentally related wordless stories.

ADDITIONAL DESERT BOOKS: *The Desert* by Susan Deming (Chronicle Books), *The Hundred Year Old Cactus* by Anita Holmes (Four Winds Press), *Animals of the Desert* by J.L. Cloudsley-Thompson (McGraw-Hill), *Animals of the Deserts* by Sylvia A. Johnson (Lerner).

©1993 Monday Morning Books, Inc.

LOVE THE EARTH!

EARTHMAKER HAND

Teacher's Note:
The Desert Is Theirs incorporates the Papago's theory of creation, which says that the Earthmaker made the desert from a dab of dirt in which a small greasewood bush grew. The following craft allows children to make a plaster hand print while exploring the ideas of people from another culture.

Materials:
Plaster of Paris (alternatives: clay or baker's dough), plastic plate or tray (one per child), sand or dirt (a small handful per child), tempera paint in desert colors (sienna, brown, green, gold), paintbrushes, dried grass, glue.

Directions:
1. To make hand prints, mix a batch of plaster of Paris according to directions on package. Pour mixture into individual plastic plates or trays. When plaster becomes firm enough to take an impression (about 10 to 15 minutes), have each child press one hand, palm-side down, into the plaster. Allow the hand prints to dry (about 45 minutes) before gently flexing the sides of the dish to remove.
2. Have children paint their prints in desert hues.
3. Students spread a bit of glue into the palm of the hand print and sprinkle in a small amount of sand or dirt.
4. Tiny clumps of grass can be glued into the base of the palm to represent a greasewood bush.

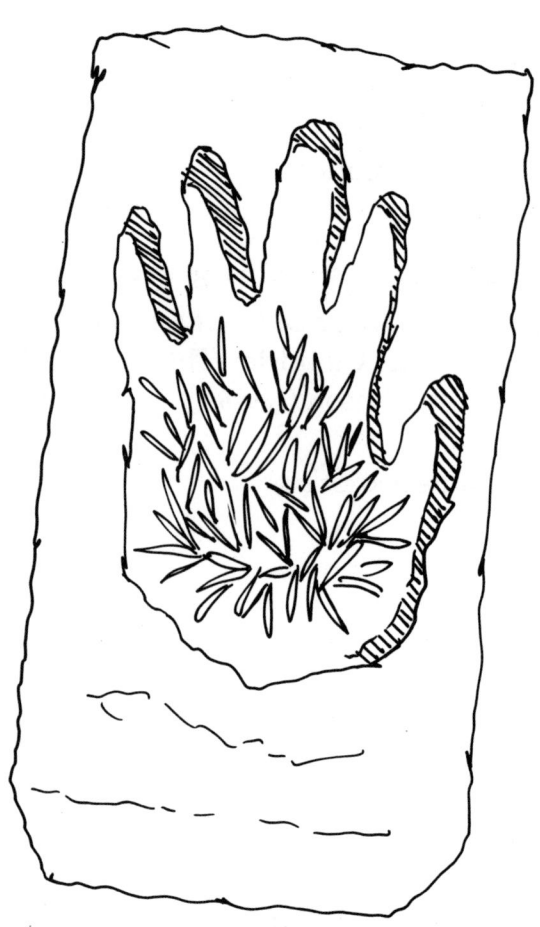

©1993 Monday Morning Books, Inc.

OVER IN THE MEADOW

Story:
Ezra Jack Keats' beautiful illustrations bring meadowland animals into your classroom. Children will quickly grasp the story's pattern and have fun repeating the verses. *Over in the Meadow* describes both the kinds of animals found in a meadow, and the different types of "homes" that a single meadow can offer. The turtles live in the sand (usually at the mouth of a stream), the muskrats live in the reeds, and birds and bees live in trees.

Environmental Connection:
Although a light-hearted tale, *Over in the Meadow* can be an enlightening aid that shows students how many species rely on a single environment. Have children brainstorm other species that might share the meadow with the animals named in the book. Additional animals might include rabbits, field mice, ladybugs, squirrels, and deer.

Language Extension:
Think up additional verses
(similar to the new ones listed below):

Over in the meadow
Where the jasmine smells like heaven,
Lived a mother bunny rabbit
And her bunnies—
Wow! Eleven!

"Hop!" said the mother.
"We hop," said eleven.
So they jumped and they hopped,
In a jasmine-scented heaven.

SAMPLE RHYMING WORDS

One: fun, none, run, sun, won.
Two: blue, do, few, grew, new.
Three: bee, free, knee, me, see.
Four: chore, door, floor, more, store.
Five: alive, chive, dive, drive, hive.
Six: chicks, fix, mix, picks, sticks.
Seven: eleven, heaven.
Eight: ate, gate, great, state, wait.
Nine: dine, fine, line, shine, vine.
Ten: den, hen, men, pen, when.

ADDITIONAL MEADOW BOOKS: *Matthew's Meadow* by Corinne Demas Bliss (Harcourt), *Secrets in the Meadow* by Lilo Hess (Scribner's).

©1993 Monday Morning Books, Inc.

FIREFLY FUN

Teacher's Note:
The final stanza in *Over in the Meadow* describes a glimmering family of fireflies. To give children an in-depth look at these lovely, illuminated critters, read aloud books such as *The Fireflies* by Max Bolliger (Atheneum), *Fireflies!* by Julie Brinckloe (Macmillan), *Fireflies in the Night* by Larry Callen (Dutton), or *Fireflies* by Bernice Kohn (Prentice-Hall). Then create a firefly haven for students to enjoy even in the daytime.

Materials:
Black and yellow construction paper, hole punch, white and metallic crayons that show on a dark background, cellophane, scissors, glue, tape.

Directions:
1. Have students punch a random pattern of holes into a piece of black construction paper. Each individual hole will represent a firefly's "tail light."
2. Children draw a bug body and head connected to each hole.
3. Students cut little circles or strips of cellophane and glue them to the firefly body to represent wings.
4. The rest of the paper becomes a night sky after students glue on a yellow construction paper circle for a moon and color in gold and silver stars with crayons.
5. Tape the firefly masterpieces onto a window. Sunshine, coming through the punched holes, will light up the black paper nights with firefly magic!

©1993 Monday Morning Books, Inc.

A RIVER RAN WILD

Story:
Lynne Cherry's *A River Ran Wild* (Harcourt) journeys back in time to when the Massachusetts' Nashua River was first discovered by Algonquin-speaking Indians. This group named the river for its clarity, calling it the "Nash-a-way," or "river with the pebbled bottom." The tribe respected nature: the river, the land, and forest. However, during the Industrial Revolution, factories polluted the river. No longer were its waters clear. Luckily, within recent decades, caring environmentalists have brought the Nashua's plight to the public's attention. Today the river is clean once again—and pebbles shine brightly from its depths.

Environmental Connection:
This story dramatizes the idea that people can work together to clean up the environment. *A River Ran Wild* helps children see that their personal ecological efforts can make a real difference. What message is more empowering than that?

Language Extension:
The history of place names is fascinating. Students may be interested in learning the origins of place names that they're familiar with: states, cities, rivers, lakes, streets, and even buildings. Have children guess the origins of names before conducting research. Sources of information include geographical and standard dictionaries, local historical societies, and interviews with long-time citizens. Examples include: Michigan (Algonquin for "great water"), Minnesota (Sioux for "milky blue water"), Mississippi (Algonquin for "big river"), New York (borrowed from York, England), and Redwood City, California (named for its once plentiful trees).

ADDITIONAL RIVER BOOKS: *The River* by David Bellamy (Crown), *Where the River Begins* by Thomas Locker (Dial), *The River Bank* by Kenneth Grahame (Scribner's), *A River Dream* by Allen Say (Houghton Mifflin).

©1993 *Monday Morning Books, Inc.*

LOVE THE EARTH!

RIVER DISPLAYS

Teacher's Note:
A River Ran Wild provides many facts about rivers in general, and the Nashua River in particular. The story allows students to see a river's importance to factories and industries, as well as to the animals who live by the river or in nearby forests. This project allows students to create their own yarn rivers, and to make up appropriate names for their imaginary waterways.

Materials:
Blue yarn, glue, old magazines, scissors, white construction paper, crayons, non-toxic markers.

Directions:
1. Have each student glue a piece of blue yarn (to represent a river) lengthwise down the center of white construction paper. Children can make their rivers straight or curvy, depending on how they position the yarn.
2. Students decide on where their river is located. Some may choose to place their river in modern times, and to draw pictures of factories or cities along the banks. Others may decide to place their river in the time of the Native Americans, before settlers developed the land. Children can use magazines, crayons, and markers to decorate their rivers.
3. After the students have finished their pictures, ask them to think up descriptive names for their rivers.
4. Write the river names along the bottom of the pictures, and post the finished projects on a Classroom Rivers bulletin board.

©1993 Monday Morning Books, Inc.

THE GREAT KAPOK TREE

Story:
Lynne Cherry's *The Great Kapok Tree* (Harcourt) describes life in an Amazon rain forest. Treetop birds live in the rain forest's sunny canopy. These colorful creatures include yellow orioles, blue fruit-eaters, multicolored toucans, scarlet macaws, and purple honeycreepers. The trees also house sloths, monkeys, and chimpanzees. Other animals, like snakes and jaguars, thrive in dim light. Their rain forest home is known as the "understory." All of these animals get together and explain to a young man why he should not cut down one of the forest's lovely Kapok trees. They speak to him (while he naps next to his axe) about the consequences of destroying the tree. Their arguments work on his sleeping mind, and upon waking, he leaves the forest empty-handed.

Environmental Connection:
Animals talk in *The Great Kapok Tree*. The porcupines explain how the trees produce oxygen. The monkeys describe how the forest might become a barren desert. A bee tells how all living things depend on one another. These important lessons are told at a child's level.

Language Extension:
The man who begins to cut down the Kapok tree changes his mind after listening to many strong arguments. Have students brainstorm a time when they may have first felt one way, and then changed their minds and felt another way. Examples: perhaps they didn't think they liked a type of food until someone convinced them to try it. Or they might not have wanted to move to a new town. Have children discuss what helped them change their minds.

ADDITIONAL RAIN FOREST BOOKS: *Rainforest* by Helen Cowcher (Farrar), *One Day in the Tropical Rain Forest* by Jean Craighead George (Thomas Y. Crowell), *Animals of the Tropical Forests* by Sylvia A. Johnson (Lerner).

©1993 Monday Morning Books, Inc.

LOVE THE EARTH!

RAIN FOREST MUSIC

Teacher's Note:
After reading *The Great Kapok Tree*, your students will have an idea of what rain forests look like. But they still won't know how they sound!

Tape recordings now exist of many environments. Even city dwellers can enjoy sounds from the ocean, desert, meadow, or rain forest. Students who may never get the chance to visit a real rain forest and hear the calls of the different birds and animals can listen to these sounds right in the classroom. You can find tapes of environments during different seasons and featuring all sorts of meteorological events: storms (light and heavy rains, thunder and lightning storms), or winds (soft breezes to blustering gales).

Materials:
Rain forest recordings such as *A Month in the Brazilian Rainforest* (RYKO), construction paper, tape recorder, crayons.

Directions:
1. Play a recording of sounds from a rain forest.
2. Have students draw images of what they are hearing.
3. Share these rain forest pictures with the rest of the school by posting them on a hallway bulletin board. Or bind the pictures together in an illustrated rain forest book, and include facts from *The Great Kapok Tree* on each page.

Option:
Have students make a tape of their own environment. They could choose different times of day to record: recess, story hour, etc. Try trading sound tapes with students from a different area. An urban class might swap city sounds for a recording of country sounds made by children in a rural area. Additional materials needed: microphone, blank tape.

©1993 Monday Morning Books, Inc.

THE LITTLE HOUSE

Story:
The Little House by Virginia Lee Burton (Houghton Mifflin) follows its main character (the Little House) through many years. At first, it lives in the country where it can observe the changing of the seasons. As time goes on, land development takes place. The city moves closer and closer, eventually surrounding the Little House. The Little House is sad when it can no longer identify the seasons, and wants to return to the country. Luckily, the Little House is discovered by the builder's great-great-granddaughter. This savvy woman hires movers to carry the Little House back to the country where it can be happy again.

Environmental Connection:
This story describes the growth of a large city. It's an important book both for children in cities who may have no concept of what came before the skyscrapers, and for children in rural areas who aren't familiar with urban life. Discuss with your students the fact that although the Little House did not like living in a town, people enjoy city life for many different reasons.

Language Extension:
Divide your class into small groups. Have them make lists of reasons to live in the country and reasons to live in the city. You can begin this activity by brainstorming (or webbing) some ideas together. Children who have visited big cities or pastoral settings can share their experiences.

City Benefits:
Cities often have more cultural offerings such as museums, zoos, concerts, plays, and movie theaters.

Rural Benefits:
Rural areas are known for having cleaner air. Citizens often experience a greater sense of bonding with their neighbors. The change of the seasons may be more apparent in areas that have abundant trees and less pollution.

©1993 Monday Morning Books, Inc.

LOVE THE EARTH!

3-D CITY AND COUNTRY MURALS

Teacher's Note:
Your students become city dwellers when they create city murals, and country dwellers when they draw pastoral murals.

Materials:
Two large sheets of butcher paper, crayons, tempera paints and brushes, non-toxic markers, empty cereal boxes (one per student), glue, scissors, construction paper.

Directions:
1. Have children work together to plan two murals: one city, and one country.
2. Students draw the murals using non-toxic markers, crayons, or tempera paints.
3. Have each child draw a house onto a piece of construction paper.
4. Students decorate their houses, cut them out, and glue them onto the cereal boxes.
5. Complete the murals by having children glue their houses onto the city or country pictures.

Option:
Children may wish to make murals representing the different seasons. Have them show what the seasons look like in both the country and the city.

©1993 Monday Morning Books, Inc.

SCAVENGER HUNT

Teacher's Note:
This activity is perfect for field trips to parks and preserves, but can also be done on a neighborhood "nature walk." Challenge children to look for items like flowers, seedpods, birds' nests, and different types of leaves. (Most will be easier to find during the fall and spring than in the winter.) Drawing pictures, rather than picking up or removing the objects, preserves the natural environment.

Materials:
Nature checklist (pages 18-19), crayons or non-toxic markers, paper.

Directions:
1. Children locate the required items, and draw a picture of each object they find.
2. Upon returning to the classroom, students share their drawings with each other. Expect many possible "correct" answers for each listed item.
3. Have children compare their drawings to discover leaves, bugs, trees, flowers, or animals that they may have missed seeing firsthand.

©1993 Monday Morning Books, Inc.

LOVE THE EARTH!

NATURE HUNT CHECKLIST 1

Try to find a match for each picture. Make your own drawings of the ones you find.

Name:

Date:

Season:

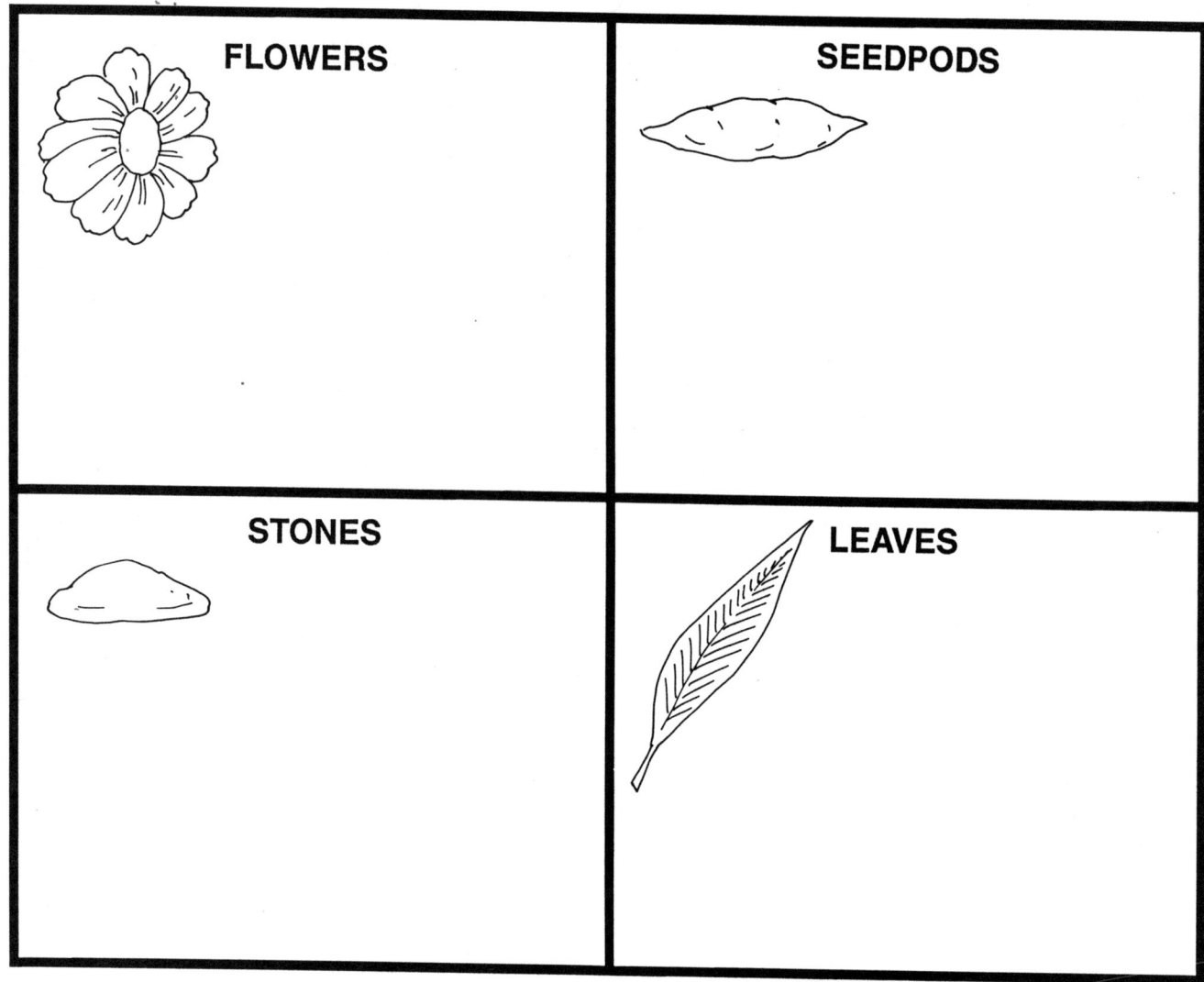

©1993 Monday Morning Books, Inc.

18

LOVE THE EARTH!

NATURE HUNT CHECKLIST 2

Try to find a match for each picture. Make your own drawings of the ones you find.

Name:

Date:

Season:

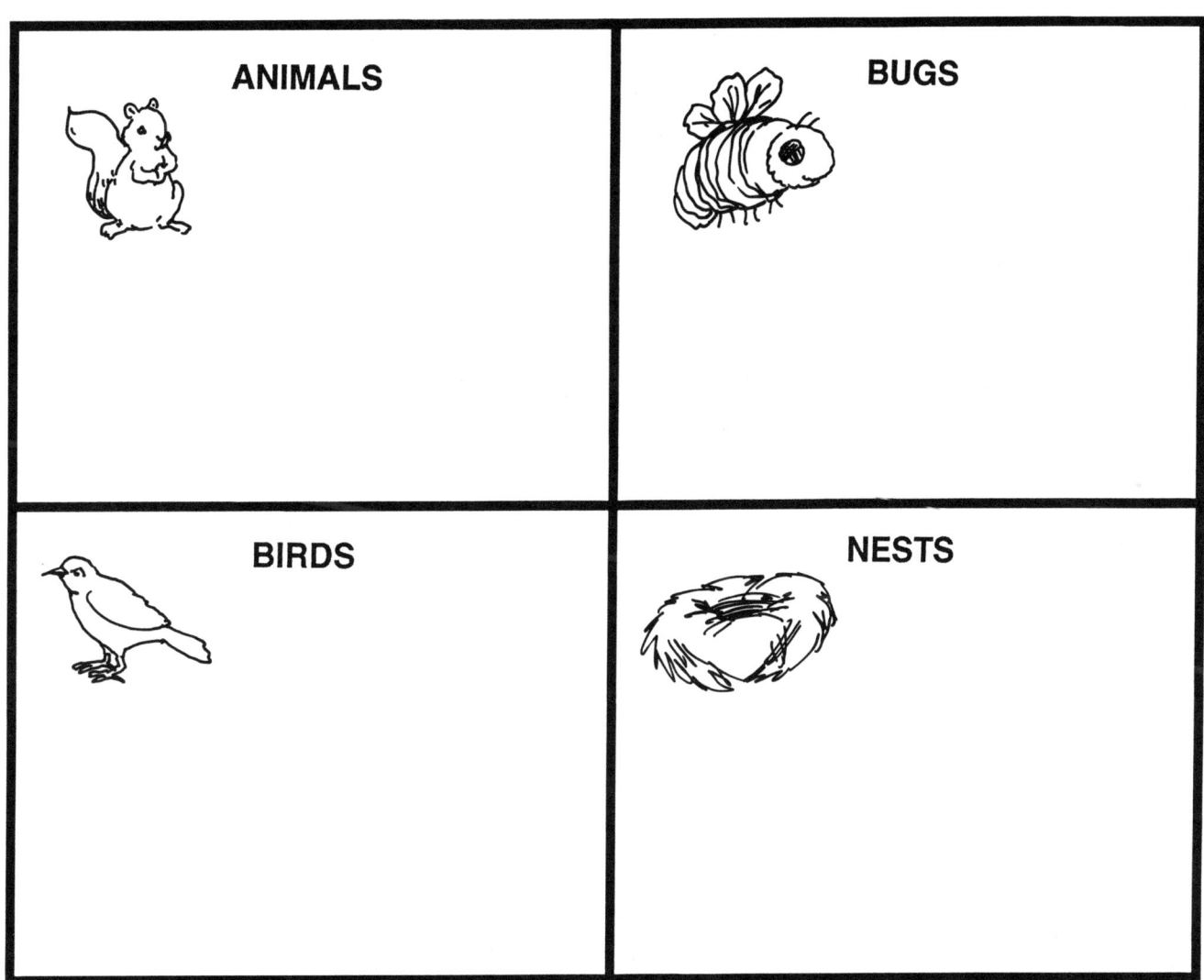

©1993 Monday Morning Books, Inc.

LOVE THE EARTH!

EROSION EXPLORATION

Teacher's Note:
The following experiment lets students explore the rate at which soil absorbs water. Children can work together on this project, taking turns doing the different steps. The quantities of materials listed are for groups of three children.

Materials:
Three tin cans with both ends removed (soup cans work well), three flowerpots (one filled with soil, the second with sand, and the third with clay dirt), empty milk carton, water, watch with a second hand, paper and pencils.

Directions:
1. Have one student push a can (end down) into each flowerpot, so that a small part is under the soil.
2. The second child should fill the can to the top with water poured quickly from the milk carton.
3. The third student times how long it takes for the water to soak in, while one partner records the information.
4. Children should repeat the procedure using the various materials. (This allows each member of the team to perform each task.)
5. Have student groups compare the results of the different tests. Which areas will best withstand erosion? Where will the water run off?

Option:
Grass, shrubs, and other plants can help the soil hold water. Are there areas in your school where more plants could be used? If so, brainstorm ways to save up money to buy more plants.

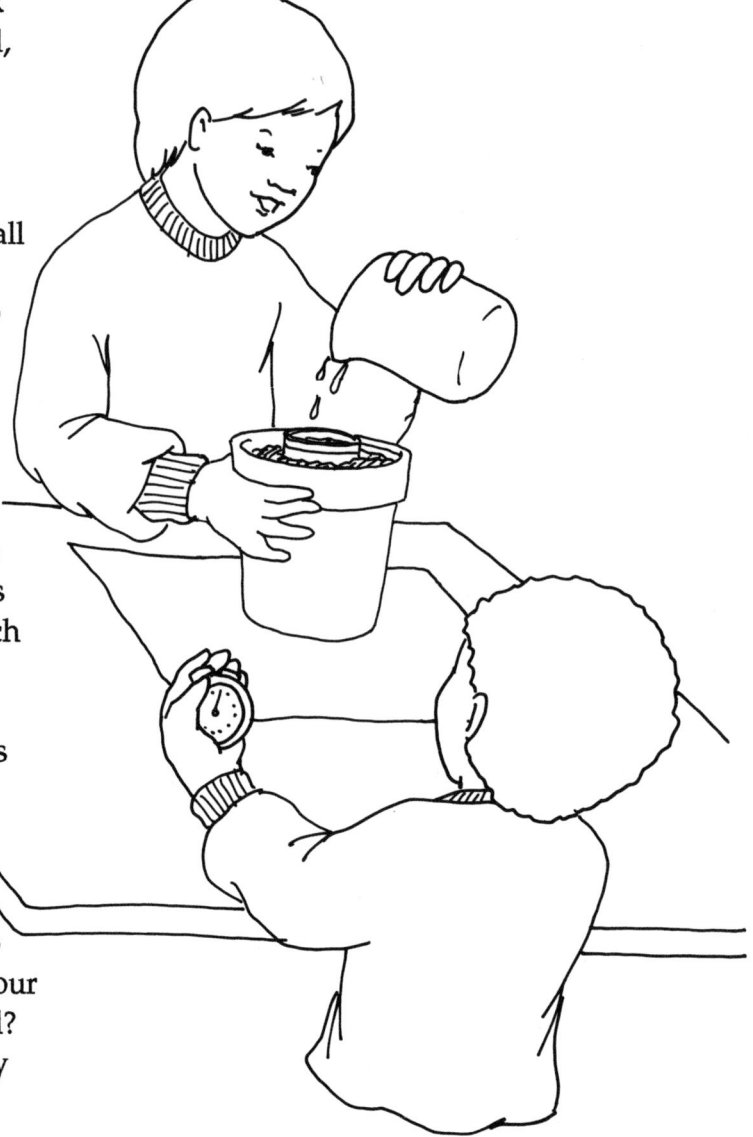

©1993 Monday Morning Books, Inc.

CONSERVATION COUNTS

Teacher's Note:
This at-home project takes at least two weeks. Each day for the first week, children will use the "Conservation Counts" fill-in chart to study their personal level of conservation consciousness. Remind students during the week that they should be keeping track of their responses every day. Compare results the following Monday, and make a large chart showing how well the class responded.

Send the chart home again for the second week. Now that the children are aware of their routines, they should more easily move toward ecological goals. On the following Monday, record the children's responses. Then compare the results of the first week to those of the second. Has your class improved?

Materials:
Conservation counts chart (page 22), crayons.

Directions:
1. Children monitor their pro-environment behaviors by marking appropriate boxes on the chart, for example: turning off the water while brushing their teeth, or biking to a friend's house instead of being driven.
2. At the end of the week, have students bring their charts in for sharing.
3. Encourage children to think of other ways to save energy and help in the fight to save the planet. Brainstorm new activities to add to their charts for the next week (some classes may wish to continue to use the charts throughout the year).
4. Students should keep each chart as it is filled up. Bind all of the charts into a "How We Helped the Planet" classroom book.

©1993 Monday Morning Books, Inc.

LOVE THE EARTH!

CONSERVATION COUNTS CHART

RECYCLE RECYCLE RECYCLE	SUNDAY	MONDAY	TUESDAY	WEDNESDAY	THURSDAY	FRIDAY	SATURDAY
💡							
🚰							
🚴							
🚗							
📚							
🧺							

©1993 Monday Morning Books, Inc.

SAVE THE AIR

Teacher's Note:
Planting a tree is a fun and inspiring activity that helps to improve the environment. The tree will reduce the carbon dioxide in the air, provide shade, and attract wildlife.

Choose a spot that has the right amount of sunlight and proper soil drainage—the tree shouldn't be too wet or dry. If you can't find a satisfactory location for a tree at school, consider planting small shrubs or bushes. Make sure to pick a tree or plant that's right for your area. Native species are best. Consult with a local nursery or environmental group. Or write for a guide from:

Tree People
12601 Mulholland Drive
Beverly Hills, CA 90210

National Arbor Day Foundation
100 Arbor Avenue
Nebraska City, NE 68410
(They offer a teacher's guide for grades 1-3.)

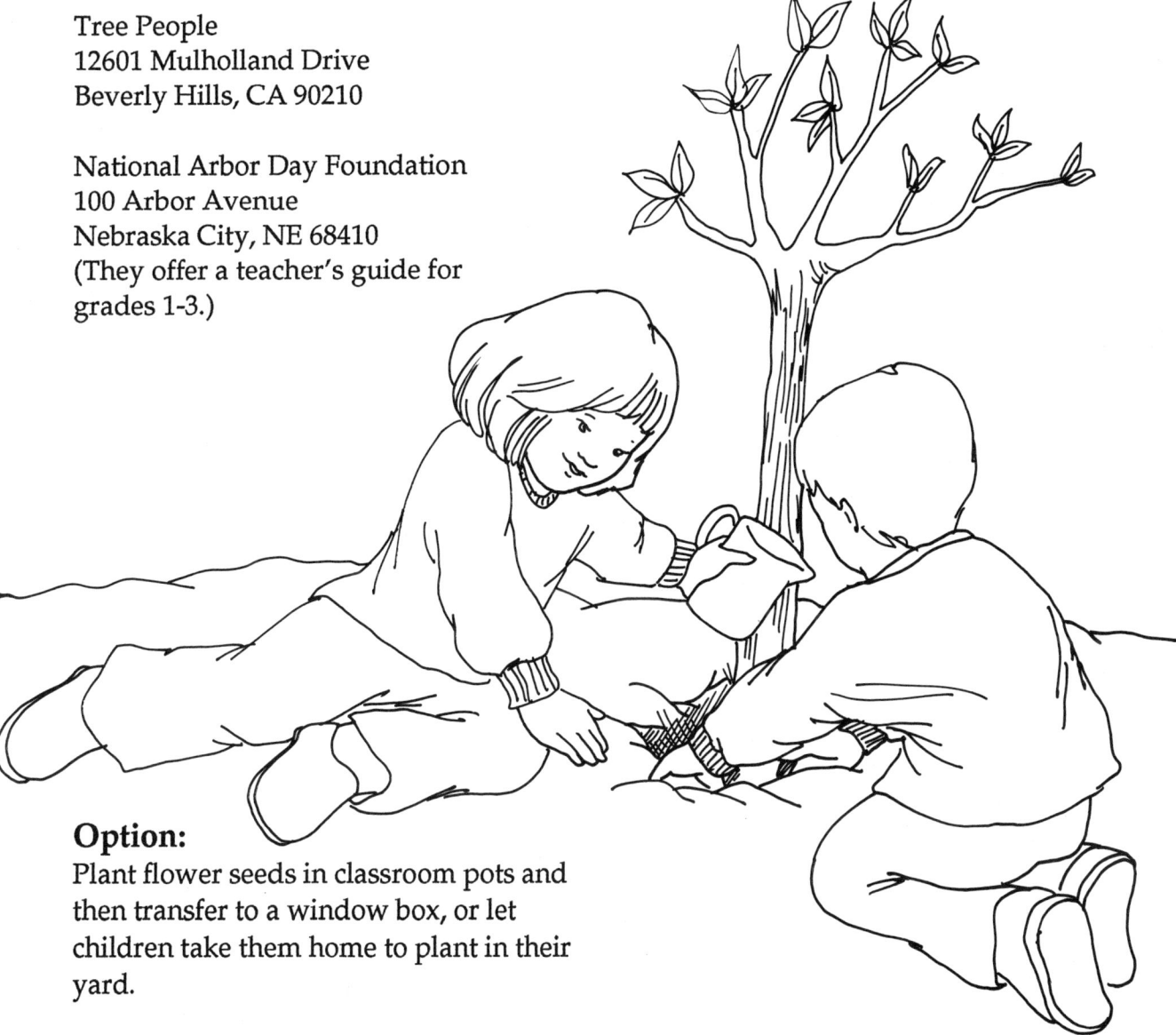

Option:
Plant flower seeds in classroom pots and then transfer to a window box, or let children take them home to plant in their yard.

©1993 *Monday Morning Books, Inc.*

LOVE THE EARTH!

WHAT THE RAIN FOREST KNOWS

Teacher's Note:
This project allows children to use their knowledge to teach others. Post this bulletin board in the library where other classes will be able to appreciate and learn from the information your students have presented.

Materials:
Poster board, colored construction paper, scissors, glue, crayons or non-toxic markers, rain forest animal patterns (page 25), fact sheet (page 26), sequins, fabric scraps, tape.

Directions:
1. Draw a large tree shape onto a piece of poster board for the students to use as a base for their bulletin board.
2. Allow children to choose an animal from the rain forest patterns. (Students may also want to find library books about rain forest animals.)
3. Each child studies the picture of the given animal, and then draws a larger reproduction onto construction paper.
4. Students cut out and decorate their animals using crayons, markers, sequins, and fabric scraps.
5. Tape the top of each child's drawing to the appropriate part of the poster board tree (so that it can be lifted).
6. Glue the corresponding fact beneath each animal.
7. Now, children can learn more about rain forest creatures by lifting the animal drawings and reading the facts below.

©1993 Monday Morning Books, Inc.

RAIN FOREST ANIMAL PATTERNS

LOVE THE EARTH!

RAIN FOREST FACTS

CANOPY	CANOPY	CANOPY
Animal: The Imperial Amazon Parrot. **Fact:** This bird has purple breast feathers, and green and red wings. Its head is blue, green, purple, and brown.	**Animal:** Vampire Bat. **Fact:** The bat cruises the forest at night in search of sleeping mammals to eat. Some bats eat moths and others insects.	**Animal:** Three-toed Sloth. **Fact:** A three-toed sloth is like an apartment house. Ninety tiny creatures can live on one of these animals.
TREE	**TREE**	**TREE**
Animal: Tree Frog. **Fact:** This funny looking frog has broad flat suckers on the ends of its fingers and toes.	**Animal:** Emerald Boa. **Fact:** This boa is a bright green that matches the leaves of the trees.	**Animal:** Golden Spider Monkey. **Fact:** This monkey is "hand-tailed." This means that it can grasp and hold objects with its tail the way people can hold things with their hands.
UNDERSTORY	**UNDERSTORY**	**UNDERSTORY**
Animal: Harvest Mouse. **Fact:** This tiny mouse has huge dark eyes for seeing at night. It is not much bigger than the raspberries it likes to eat.	**Animal:** Hercules Beetle. **Fact:** This beetle is the size of a baseball. It has finger-sized pincers, and looks like a knight in armor.	**Animal:** Ocelot. **Fact:** This pretty hunter is a fierce member of the cat family.

©1993 Monday Morning Books, Inc.

SAGUARO CACTUS TIME LINE

Teacher's Note:
The Saguaro (pronounced "Sa-wa-ro") Cactus can live for over 100 years. Imagine all that has happened in the lifetime of a cactus that began to grow in 1900! Introduce this project by creating a large cactus time line on the chalkboard (as shown). Help children fill in different important events and inventions from over the past 100 years. Examples: the moon landing, and the first airplane, car, television, telephone, Hula Hoop, and movie projector. Students can gather the data by interviewing family members, neighbors, and other teachers.

Materials:
Personal time line (page 28; one for each child), crayons, old magazines, scissors, glue.

Directions:
1. Help students brainstorm skills that they've mastered, places they've visited, or major family events. Examples include learning to ride a bike, going to Disneyland, buying a pet, the birth of a sibling, and learning to read.
2. Students then draw pictures of the above items, or glue related magazine cutouts onto their cactus time lines.
3. Children could use an assortment of cactus time lines to record different types of events: school achievements, personal successes, and family events.
4. Have children share their time lines with each other.
5. Share your own time line with the children. They may set personal goals on the basis of some of your achievements.

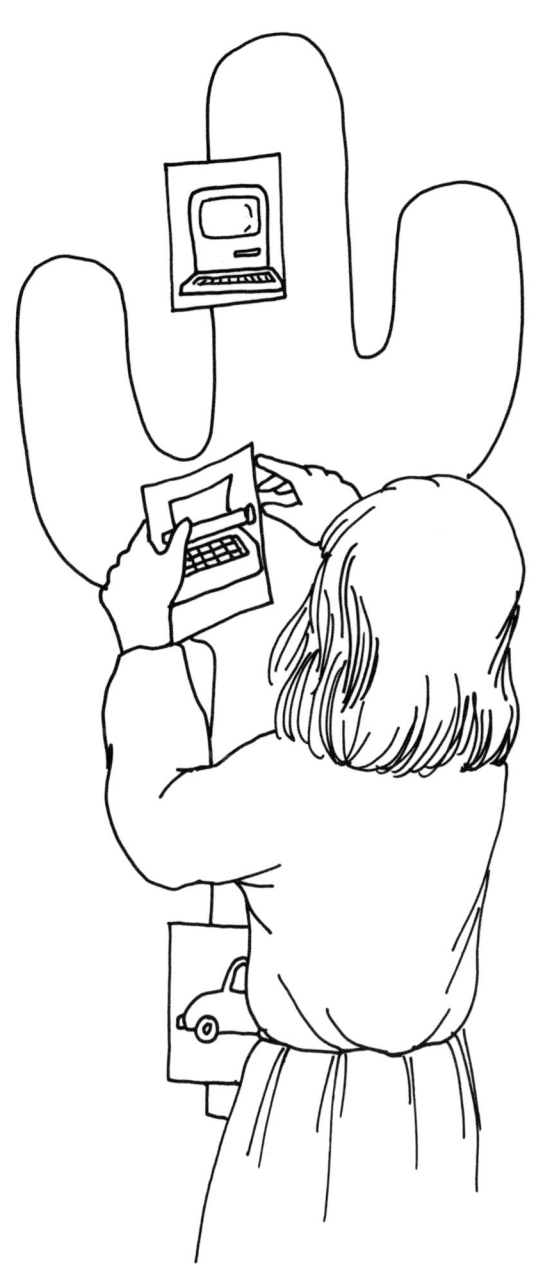

©1993 Monday Morning Books, Inc.

LOVE THE EARTH!

PERSONAL TIME LINE

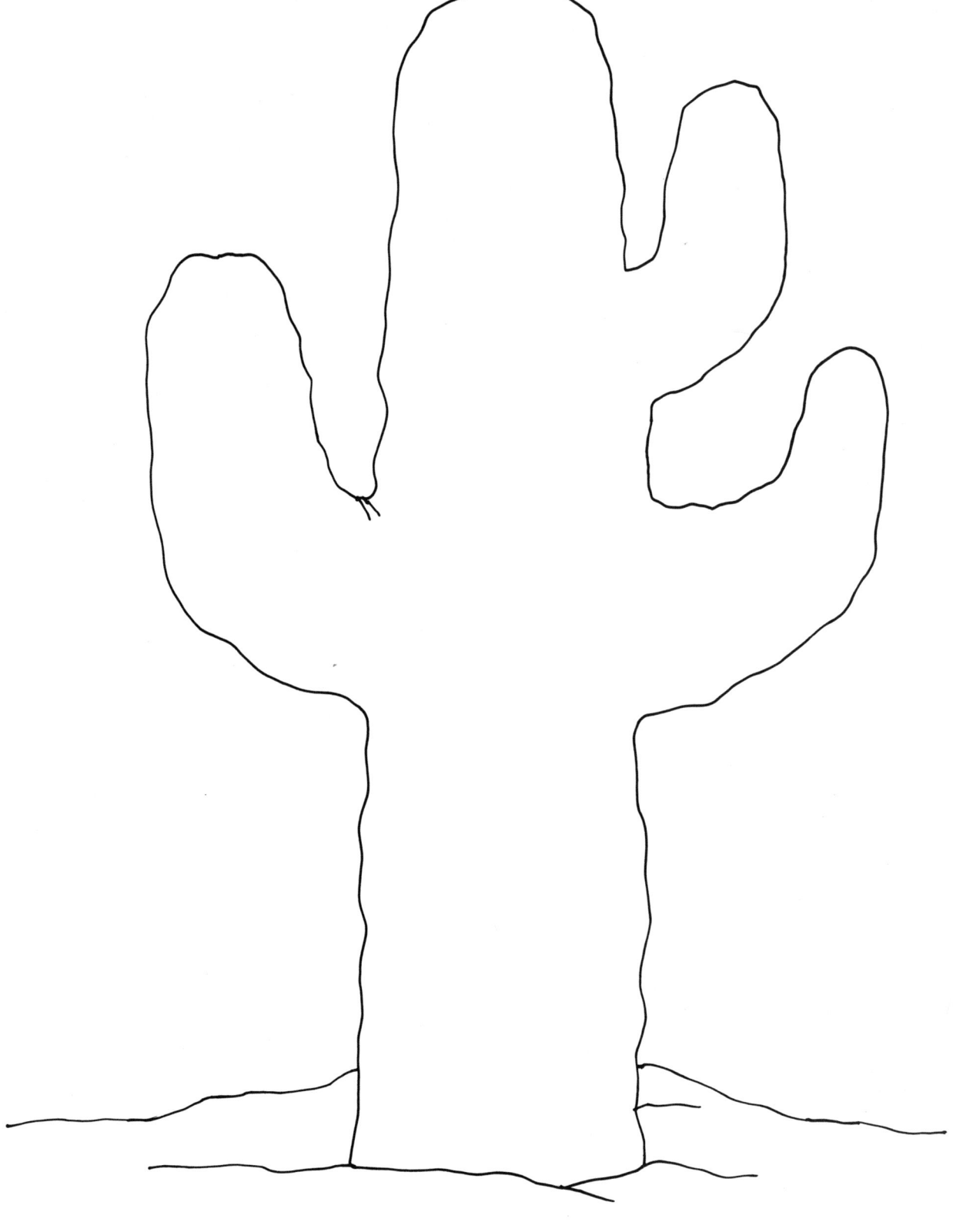

©1993 Monday Morning Books, Inc.

MEADOW MEMENTOS MOBILE

Teacher's Note:
This mobile project celebrates natural things children might observe while visiting a meadow. Examples include stalks of wheat grasses, field mice, berry bushes, leaves, or deer.

Materials:
Wire hanger, meadow patterns (page 30), yarn (in various colors), construction paper, scissors, glue, hole punch, oaktag, crayons, non-toxic markers, scraps of fabric. Optional: materials gathered on a nature walk (twigs, grass, acorns).

Directions:
1. After a field trip or a nature walk, have students draw meadow mementos on oaktag or construction paper. (Provide patterns for ideas.)
2. Children cut out their drawings. (Twigs or leaves can be tied to yarn.)
3. Students punch holes in the pieces of paper, and tie a different length of colored yarn through each hole.
4. The free yarn ends are fastened to the wire hanger to make the mobiles.
5. Children should slide the strings back and forth to balance their mobiles.
6. Hang the completed mobiles in the classroom or library.

Option:
Use the patterns to stage an indoor meadow visit. Enlarge the pictures, and glue them onto stiff cardboard. Have students decorate the pictures, and place them in different locations around your classroom. Take your children on a tour around your "meadowland" classroom.

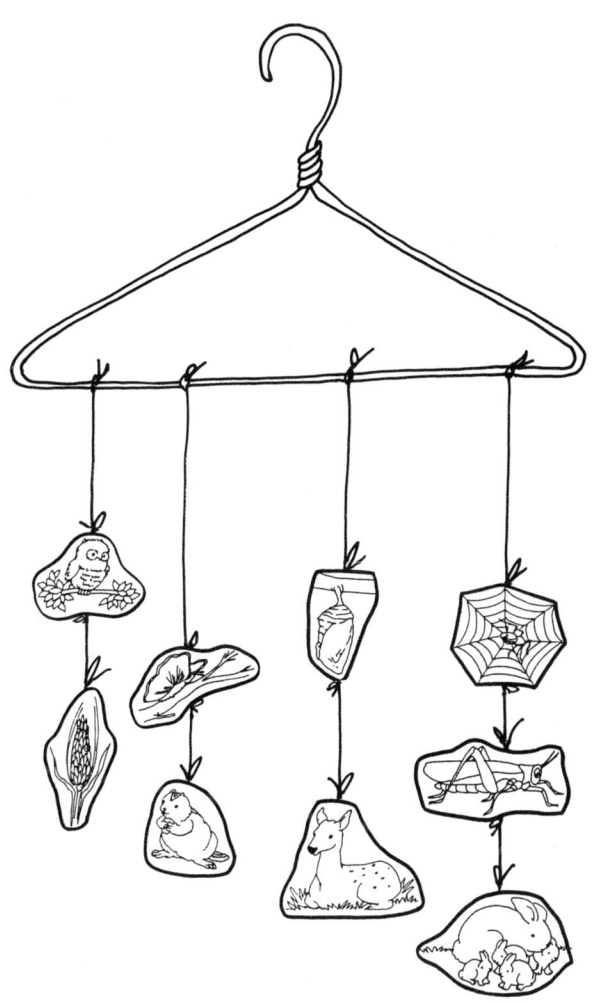

©1993 Monday Morning Books, Inc.

LOVE THE EARTH!

MEADOW PATTERNS

©1993 Monday Morning Books, Inc.

LOVE THE EARTH!

CLEAN OCEAN/DIRTY OCEAN

Teacher's Note:
The Earth's oceans were once pollution free. Now, due to the dumping of various waste matter, our seas are less pure. The following project allows children to recreate the oceans of the past, while depicting their appearance today. Students may be encouraged to join the worldwide effort to improve the health of the oceans.

Materials:
White construction paper, clear cellophane sheets (2 per child), crayons, gum wrappers, can labels, plastic six-pack rings, clean ocean patterns (page 32), dirty ocean patterns (page 33), ocean poster, glue, scissors, crayons, non-toxic markers, stapler.

Directions:
1. On the construction paper sheet, have children create an ocean background using crayons or markers to draw water.
2. Students cut out and decorate "clean" ocean patterns. Or have children study the patterns and then draw, cut out, and decorate their own versions. Children can also refer to the informative material found on the ocean poster.
3. Children glue the cut-outs onto the first cellophane sheet, making sure that the animals are in the "sea-level" section of the cellophane. When the sheet is placed over the paper sea, the animals should be in the water—not the sky.
4. Have students decorate the "dirty" ocean patterns, or draw their own versions after studying the pattern sheet.
5. Children repeat #3 using the second cellophane sheet.
6. Students glue the wrappers onto the "dirty" scene.
7. The edges of one cellophane sheet should be stapled to the left side of the paper ocean and the second sheet's edges stapled to the right side. With the first sheet folded over to cover the blue paper, the children can see a clean ocean. The second sheet shows the ocean's polluted state.
8. Have students color the coral for the clean page, and leave it blank for the unhealthy one. Coral loses its color in polluted waters.

©1993 *Monday Morning Books, Inc.*

LOVE THE EARTH!

CLEAN OCEAN PATTERNS

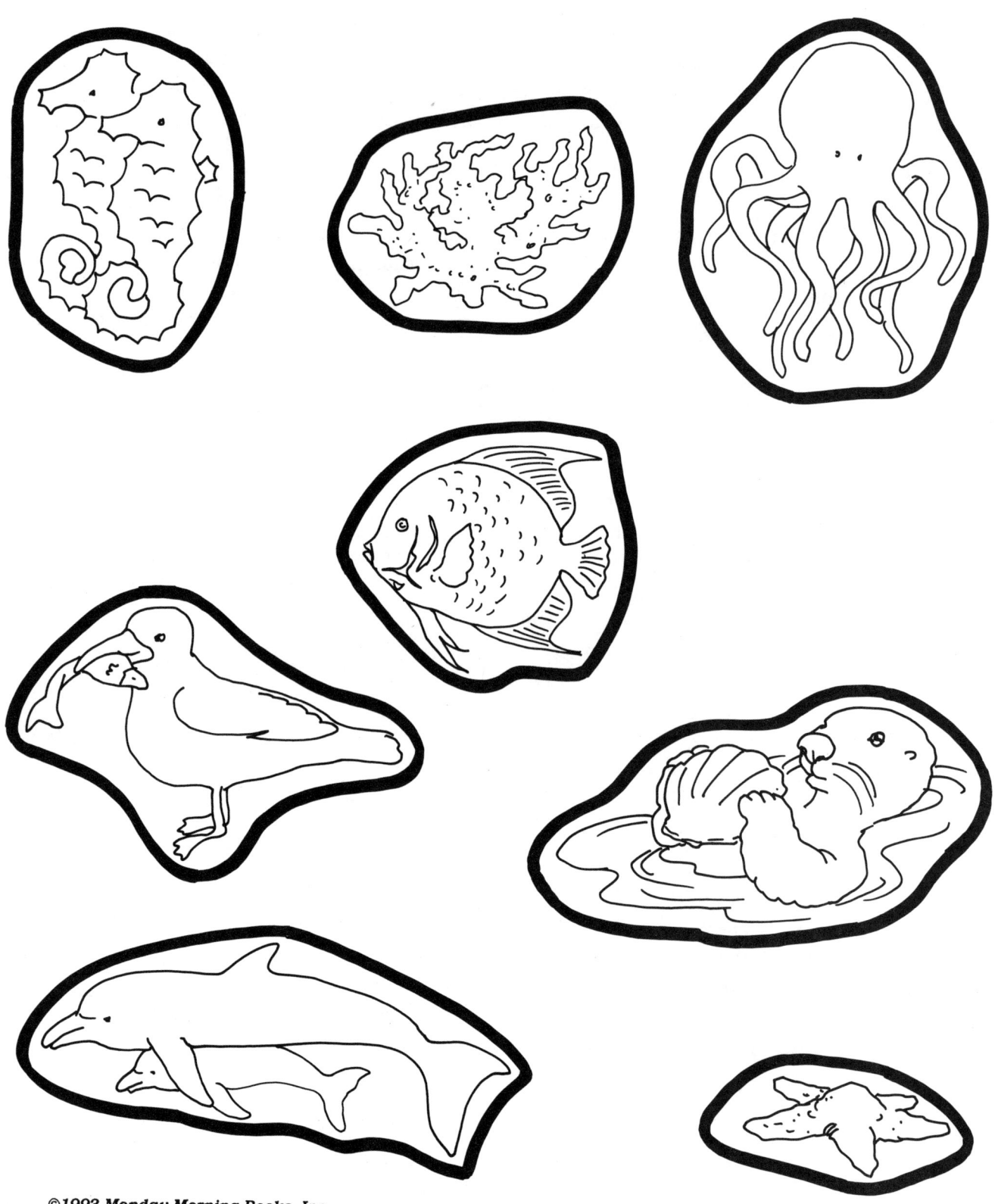

©1993 Monday Morning Books, Inc.

DIRTY OCEAN PATTERNS

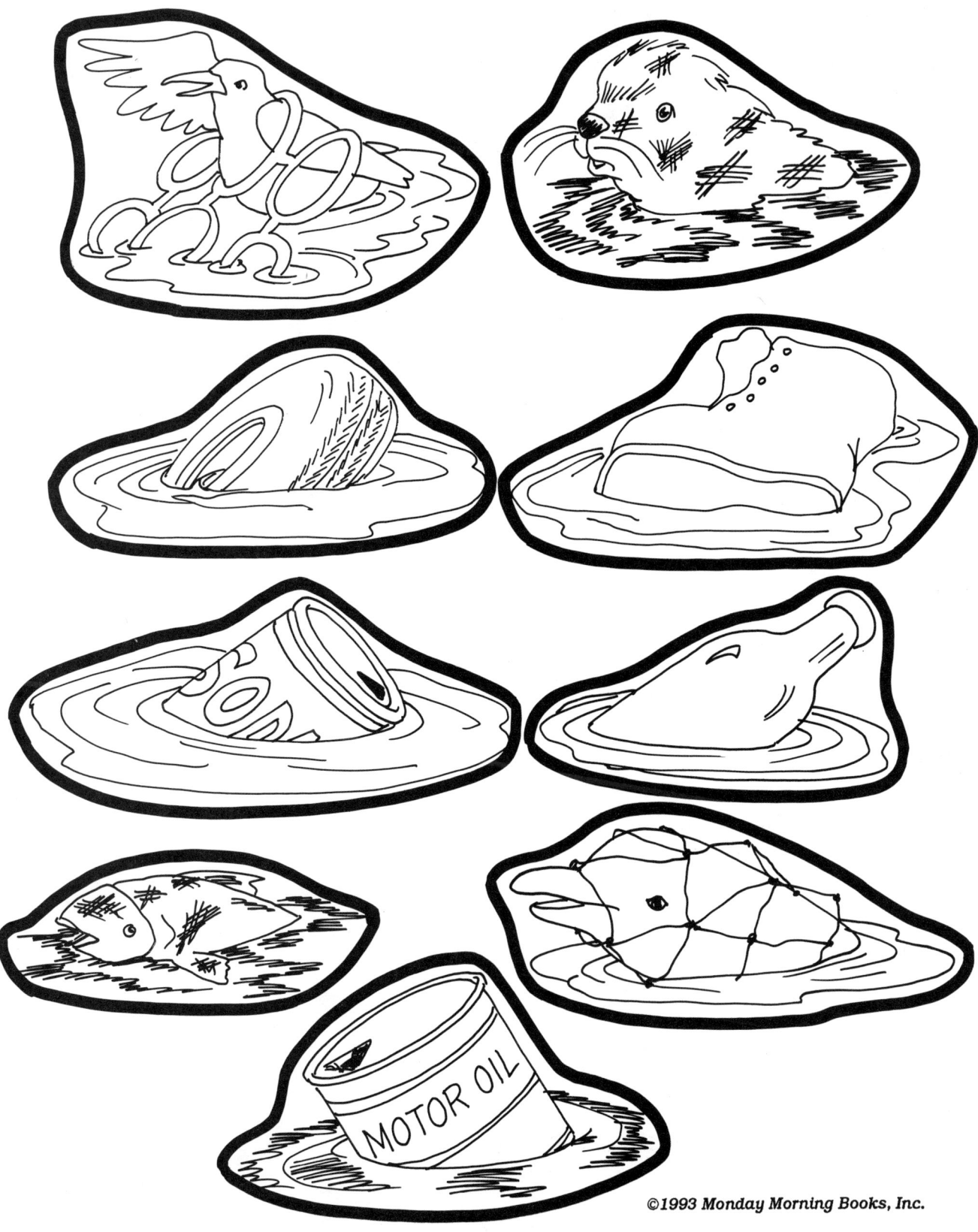

LOVE THE EARTH!

PROGRAM

The Great Saguaro Cactus
Rain Forest Rock
Over by the Water
Save the Meadowlands Hula
Grand Finale

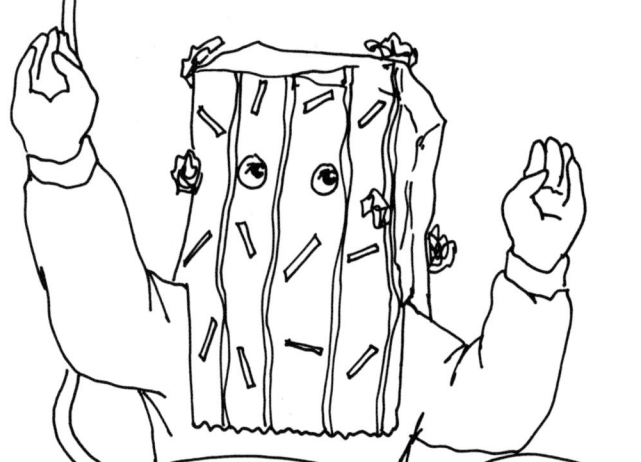

©1993 Monday Morning Books, Inc.

🎵 THE GREAT SAGUARO CACTUS

THE GREAT SAGUARO ("sa-wa-ro") CACTUS
(To the tune of "Rudolph the Red-nosed Reindeer.")

The great saguaro cactus
Grows to be so big and tall,
I wouldn't want to stand by
If it should begin to fall.

Many small desert creatures,
Live in the saguaro's stalk,
Others stop by to visit,
When they take a desert walk.

(Chorus)
Once the cactus was a seed
Buried in the sand.
It had lain for many weeks
Before the rains began.

Then the black clouds moved over,
Covering the desert sky,
And blotted out the red sun,
Bringing rain to land so dry.

(Chorus)
The small cactus seed soaked rain,
Swelled to twice its size.
Sprouted roots and tiny leaves
And soon was one inch high.

If you are in the desert
Please come stop and say "Hello."
You'll see so many creatures
Living in the saguaro!

©1993 Monday Morning Books, Inc.

CACTUS COSTUME

Teacher's Note:
Children wear this cactus costume while performing "The Great Saguaro Cactus" song (page 35). For variety, have students create different types of cacti, or cacti in bloom.

Materials:
Brown paper grocery bag (one per child), crayons or non-toxic markers, different shades of green tempera paint, paint brushes, tissue paper in floral colors (magenta, red, orange, yellow), construction paper for prickles (white, tan, beige), scissors, glue.

Directions:
1. Children cut slits in the sides of the bags, so that the costumes fit comfortably over their shoulders.
2. Help students mark their eye positions on the paper bags. (Each child can wear a bag while a partner gently marks where eye cut-outs should be with a crayon or marker.)
3. Children take their bags off and cut out the eye holes.
4. Have students paint their bags green.
5. Students cut short strips of construction paper for prickles, and glue them onto their bags. (Prickles can also be painted directly onto the costume in white or beige after the bag dries.)
6. To make a blooming cactus, children cut out circles of different colors of tissue paper, then scrunch the paper up slightly to symbolize flowers, and glue onto the costume.
7. For a realistic touch, encourage students to draw pictures of birds, insects, and desert animals to glue onto their bags.

©1993 Monday Morning Books, Inc.

RAIN FOREST ROCK

RAIN FOREST ROCK
(To the tune of "Jingle Bell Rock.")

Rain Forest, Rain Forest, Rain Forest Rock,
Rain makes plants grow.
(My teacher said so.)

Vines and tall grasses
Of vivid greens
What a healthy scene!

Rain Forest, Rain Forest, Rain Forest Rock
The rain showers
Grow perfumed flowers.

Plants in the forests
Exhale the air
Which keeps us humans here!

(Chorus)
We've decided now's the right time
So we'll clean up our act.
Won't you help us, for together,
We can launch a stronger attack!

Rain Forest, Rain Forest, Rain Forest Rock,
Let's save the Earth,
And cut fewer trees.

We'll make the planet
A safe, healthy place,
For the birds and the bees!

(Repeat chorus)

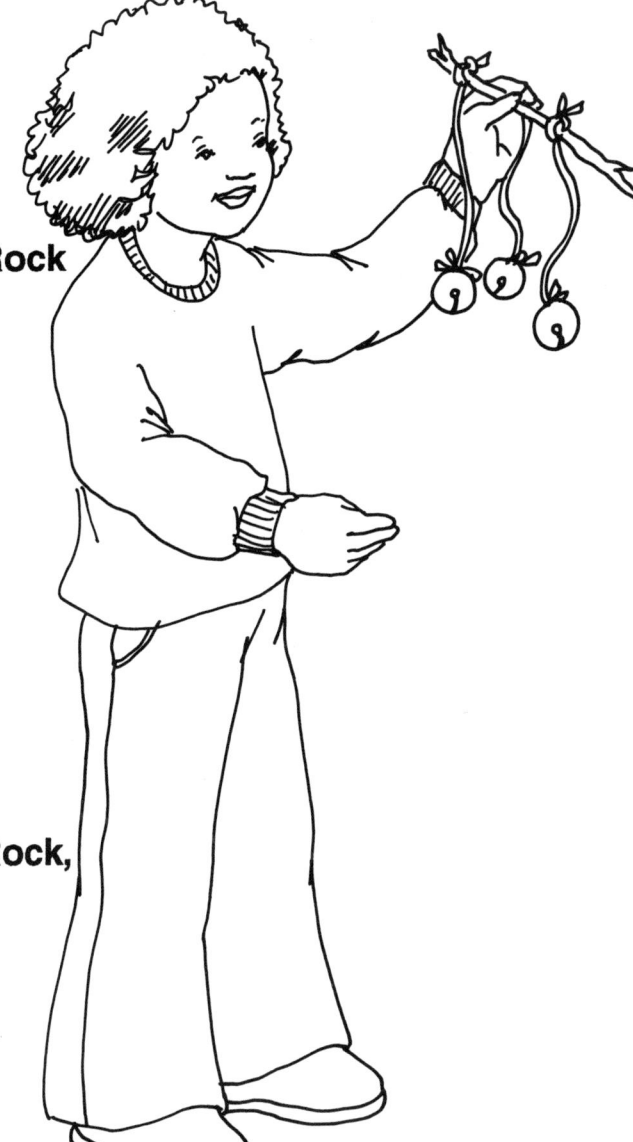

©1993 Monday Morning Books, Inc.

LOVE THE EARTH!

JINGLING BRANCHES

Teacher's Note:
Children shake jingling branches while singing and dancing to "The Rain Forest Rock" (page 37).

Materials:
Small but sturdy twigs or branches, jingle bells (with metal loops on top for fastening to yarn), short lengths of different colored yarn, glue.

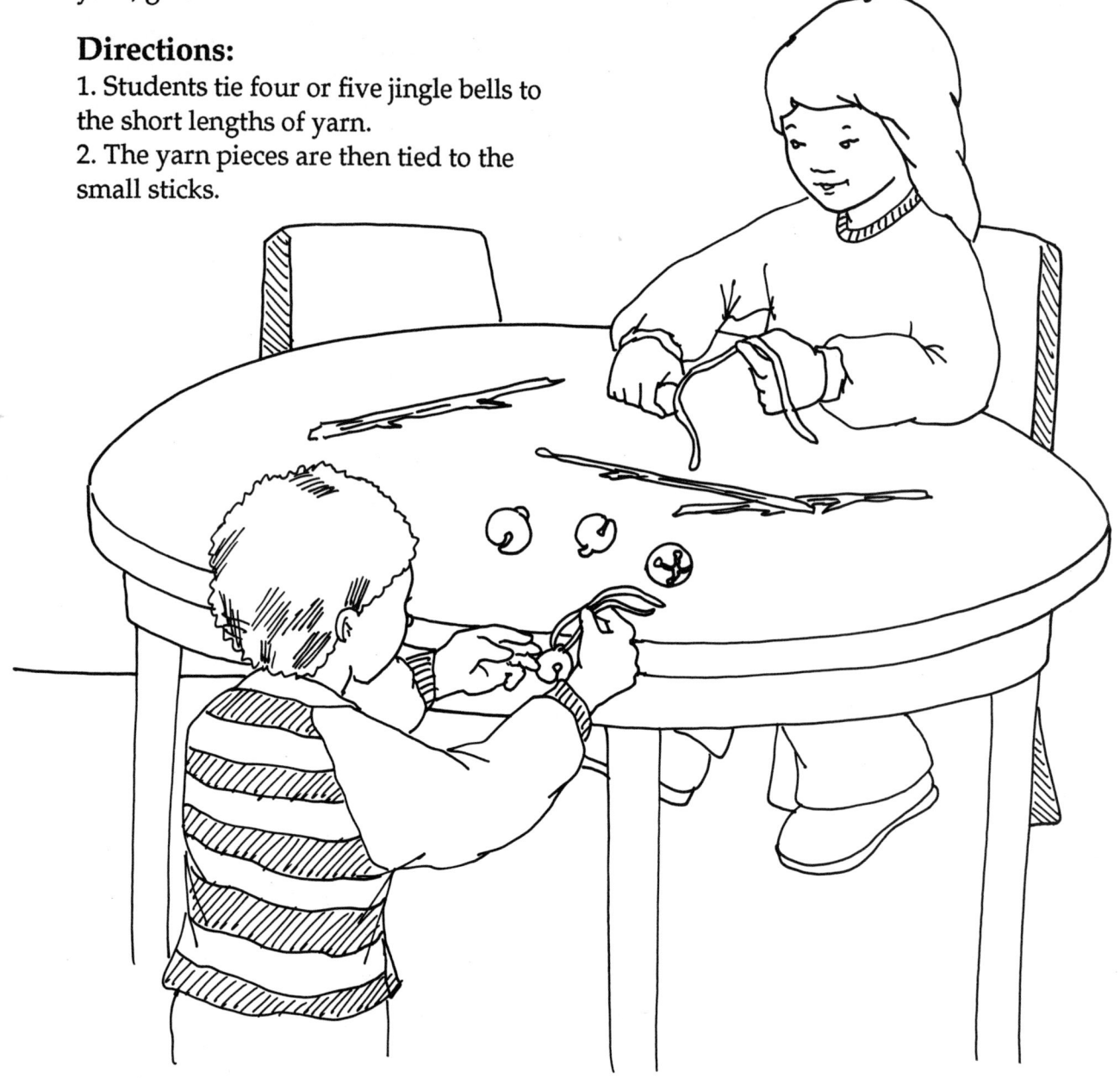

Directions:
1. Students tie four or five jingle bells to the short lengths of yarn.
2. The yarn pieces are then tied to the small sticks.

©1993 Monday Morning Books, Inc.

OVER BY THE WATER

OVER BY THE WATER
(To the tune of "Over in the Meadow.")

Over by the water,
Where the stream reflects the sun,
Lived a mother mountain lion and her small cub.
There was one.

"Roar," said the mama.
"I roar," said the one.
So they growled and they roared
Underneath the setting sun.

Over by the water,
Where both creek and sky are blue,
Lived a mama red-tailed hawk and her babies.
There were two.

"Soar," said the mother.
"We soar," said the two.
So they swooped and they soared
Through a cloudless sky of blue.

Over by the water,
Where the brook babbles with glee,
Lived a father opossum and his children.
There were three.

"Sleep," said the papa.
"We sleep," said the three.
For they only roam at night
When it's bed for you and me.

Over by the water,
Where the ocean meets the shore,
Lived a mother hermit crab and her babies.
There were four.

"Dig," said the mama.
"We dig," said the four.
So they burrowed in the sand
Near the dunes that lined the shore.

Over by the water,
Where the river is alive,
Lived a lovely mama beaver and her daughters.
There were five.

"Gnaw," said the mother.
"We gnaw," said the five.
So they chewed and they gnawed
With small teeth as sharp as knives.

©1993 Monday Morning Books, Inc.

LOVE THE EARTH!

SAVE THE MEADOWLANDS HULA

SAVE THE MEADOWLANDS HULA
(To the tune of "Everybody Do the Hukilah.")

Everybody save the meadowlands
Where grass is green, and flowers make the air smell grand.

Everybody save the meadowlands
Where streams run free, and turtles dance on banks of sand.

Please join us and save the meadowlands
This task will go much faster if you lend a hand!

Yes, we're going to the meadowlands
The meadow-meadow-meadow-meadowlands!

©1993 Monday Morning Books, Inc.

LEIS AND GRASS SKIRTS

Teacher's Note:
Girls dress in these "grass" skirts and leis while performing the "Meadowland Hula" (page 40). Boys can wear shorts. All children wear the paper leis.

GRASS SKIRTS

Materials:
Large sheets of green crepe paper or construction paper, yarn, beads (two per child), scissors, hole punch.

Directions:
1. Cut the green paper into strips lengthwise. Each child's skirt will require about 50 strips to make. These will hang loosely and flutter as the students hula.
2. Punch a hole at the top of each paper strip.
3. Measure a piece of yarn to see how much is needed to fit around each child's waist, with room to tie a bow to fasten.
4. Cut the yarn to appropriate length.
5. Have students string the strips of paper onto the length of yarn.
6. Children knot a bead at each end of the yarn to secure the paper strips.
7. When ready to perform, students tie on the skirts, fasten with a bow, and hula away!

DANDELION LEIS

Materials:
Flower patterns (page 42), construction paper in different colors, scissors, yarn lengths, sequins, glue, non-toxic markers, crayons, hole punch.

Directions:
You don't need to pick dandelions to make these leis. Simply reproduce the flower patterns. Students can study the pictures and draw their own versions, which they cut out, color, and decorate, punch two holes in, and string onto long lengths of yarn to go around their necks.

©1993 Monday Morning Books, Inc.

LOVE THE EARTH!

FLOWER PATTERNS

©1993 Monday Morning Books, Inc.

42

GRAND FINALE

LET'S SAVE THE EARTH TODAY
(To the tune of "Ding Dong the Witch is Dead.")

Let's save the meadowlands,
Rain forests,
And desert sands
Save the environment today!

(Chorus)
We'll have to work long and hard,
Pick up trash,
Clean our yards.
Let's fix up our planet today!

We'll learn to recycle,
Use things twice,
And precycle.
Hard work will save the Earth today!

(Repeat Chorus)

©1993 Monday Morning Books, Inc.

ECO-NEWSLETTER

Teacher's Note:
Turn your students into newsletter writers, editors, and illustrators with this ongoing ecological project. The Eco-newsletter is a cooperative activity. Class members help choose which information to include. Reproduce as many of the patterns as needed to represent work by all students.

Materials:
Newsletter pattern (page 45), environmental information, writing and illustrating materials.

Directions:
1. Show your students examples of newsletters. Sample kids' newsletters can be obtained from:

The Comeback Trail
Defenders of Wildlife
1244 19th St., NW
Washington, DC 20036

Kind News (Kids In Nature's Defense)
67 Salem Rd.
East Haddam, CT 06423

2. List and explain the various departments that can make up a newsletter. Examples: editorial, local news, national news, entertainment, special events.
3. As the class learns about the environment, have students keep folders to save interesting information: ecological articles, poems, flyers, stories, pictures, and drawings.
4. Encourage children to be on the lookout for pertinent information on television or in library books. Have them write down these facts in an environmental journal.
5. Students can interview local ecological specialists. Or they can write to different environmental groups.
6. Remind students to collect information while learning about the different types of environments discussed in this book. Your class may want to devote a separate newsletter to focus on the deserts, oceans, meadowlands, or rain forests.
7. If there is a particular environmental concern plaguing your town, have students learn about that. Some cities have problems with baylands or rivers. Others have too few trees. Look into your community's well-being.
8. At the end of each month, have your students sort through all of the information, and choose items for the newsletter.
9. Include special events in your newsletter stories. Examples include: Animal Rights' Week, Anti-litter Month, Arbor Day, and Earth Day.
10. The Eco-newsletter form provides sample headings. To replace these with your own ideas, delete before copying.
11. Duplicate the newsletter to send home to parents.

Option:
Each month, put on a school Eco-TV show using material from the newsletters.

©1993 Monday Morning Books, Inc.

EYE ON THE EARTH NEWS

LOCAL NEWS

NATIONAL NEWS
✩ ✩ ✩   ✩ ✩ ✩

ENTERTAINMENT

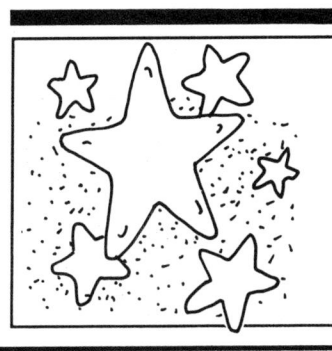

SPECIAL EVENTS

LOVE THE EARTH!

LETTER TO THE EARTH

Teacher's Note:
This activity is a variation of a time capsule. The book *Mother Earth* by Nancy Luena (Atheneum) may help children think up ideas for their letters.

Materials:
Letter Form (page 48), pens or pencils.

Directions:
1. Have children work together to think up strengths and weaknesses about the way the world is today. If this concept is too broad for your students, focus on the pros and cons about their town or school instead. List ideas in two columns on the chalkboard.
2. Encourage students to come up with ways they would like the world to change.
3. On the "Letter to the Earth" forms, have students write to our planet, giving reasons for why they are happy with its current state, and ways they feel it should be improved.
4. Copy the letters and store in a safe place for future classes to read. Or mount the letters in the library for all of the school to enjoy.
5. Have children seal their letters in envelopes that say, "To be opened when I am 21." These letters should be sent home to their parents for safekeeping. Discuss how students might feel when they read their letters as adults. How do they think the Earth will have changed? What would make them happiest? What would disappoint them?
6. Discuss what their parents or grandparents might have written if they had done this activity 20 or 40 years ago.

©1993 *Monday Morning Books, Inc.*

LOVE THE EARTH!

ADDRESSES

Teacher's Note:
Your students can write to environmental groups for information about the Earth. They can use the "Letter Form" (page 48). Have students write on the back of the letter forms, then fold, seal with tape, address, stamp, and mail.

Canadian Environmental Network
P.O. Box 1289, Station B
Ottawa, Ontario
KIP 5R3

Center for Environmental Education
1725 DeSales Street NW
Suite 500
Washington, DC 20036

The Children's Rain forest
P.O. Box 936
Lewiston, Maine 04240

Citizens for a Better Environment
942 Market Street Suite 505
San Francisco, CA 94102

Educators for Social Responsibility
23 Garden Street
Cambridge, MA 02138

Friends of the Earth
218 D Street SE
Washington, DC 20003

The Institute for Earth Education
P.O. Box 288
Warrenville, IL 60555

The Institute for Environmental Education
32000 Chagrin Blvd.
Cleveland, OH 44124

Kids Against Pollution
Tenakill School
275 High Street
Closter, NJ 07624

National Energy Foundation
Resources for Education
National Office
5160 Wiley Post Way, Suite 200
Salt Lake City, UT 884116

PhilaPride, Inc.
123 S. Broad Street Suite 1326
Philadelphia, PA 19109

Pollution Probe
12 Madison Avenue
Toronto, Ontario
M5R 2S1

Toxic Avengers
c/o El Puente
211 South Fourth Street
Brooklyn, NY 11211

Washington State Department of Ecology
Litter Control and Recycling Program
4350 150th Avenue NE
Redmond, WA 98052

©1993 Monday Morning Books, Inc.

LOVE THE EARTH!

LETTER FORM

Apply glue to flap, fold, and secure with tape or glue.
FOLD.

From:

To:

Place Stamp Here

FOLD.

©1993 Monday Morning Books, Inc.